MIXED EMOTIONS

Published by Spines
ISBN 979-8-89691-306-1

MIXED EMOTIONS

Book of Poems

____

BRITTANI NECHELLE DARENSBOURG

Contents

Introduction

ABOUT THE AUTHOR

"Full of love for poetry since I was 9 years old. God blessed me with a gift and I'm so grateful to present it to readers and poetry lovers across the world. I published my first poetry book ever, 'Love, Passion, And Betrayal" in 2024. Poetry is amazing, you can read it, imagine it, and feel it."

-Brittani Darensbourg

-Author

Part I

DAMAGED EMOTIONS

Unforgiven

You mistreated me for no reason. What a horrible experience of life in this season. I promised to give you all of me to share. To never do me wrong, you swear. In me, you had a cruel investment causes me to be full of resentment. As time flies I'm still not over your lies. Tried so hard not to judge. Yet I remain to hold a grudge. To wrath, I am driven, very unforgiven.....

By: Brittani Darensbourg

Guilt

____

know I'm wrong for what I've done. I can't change the number of things, not even one. What goes around comes around under the sun. Apologies, you didn't accept none. The pain is eating me up alive, in my heart there's no peace inside. Though I mixed lies with the truth, I fear paying for it all and everything I do. For you I wasn't well built, I'm broken and left with all the guilt.

By: Brittani Darensbourg

Regret

Thinking about moments we both loved and shared. As I lie down in bed, I look up to the ceiling and stare. In many ways I was wrong and unfair. All the pain you didn't deserve, now I'm soaked with sorrow and tears what I once served. Your love I took for granted, now I'm left lonely and stranded. I mishandled you, now someone's loving you and being true. Knowing you're never coming back, leaves me upset, and full of..... Regret.

By: Brittani Darensbourg

I'm Sorry

We been through a lot together. Even through weary weather. In many stages of hoping things will get better. You're gone and I'm left all alone. In you, I created a heart of stone. We will never see eye to eye again. Our love story is definitely a complete end. No more love to give but wishing you would forgive..... I'm sorry.

By: Brittani Darensbourg

Can't let Go

Holding on to sweet loving memories over the years that only you and I can repeat. Knowing that you don't agree, is very sad for me. Your actions now shows me you never cared, hurts my heart deep. As days, weeks, months, and years go by, I really see, that you pretend your love was real. As I sit and think I really don't know what I feel. This hurts me so and I can't let go.

By: Brittani Darensbourg

Confused

All the romance you show me leads me to ecstasy. Signs that tell me you wanna make me yours and set me free from being lonely. To my heart, you have the key. I put our situation in your hands but yet never gave me a chance. I sometimes feel that I'm not good enough. Caught up in a love game of mix signals and full potential is very rough. Me with all these feelings for you knowing we are just friends leaves my heart bruised. Someday it will be revealed, am I being used? Or am I just..... Confused?

By: Brittani Darensbourg

Unfair Love

Ialways find myself falling in love first. Some days I wonder if it's a blessing or a curse. It's me every time in the end who gets hurt. In every situation I see all your worth, but somehow you never saw mine. How you treat me flows through my mind all the time. Do you really love me? I need a sign. Feelings of being used, my emotions are in such a scare. This thing called love is so unfair.

By: Brittani Darensbourg

Fear

My thoughts run so deep, hard to pretend to be joyful and free. You are a stranger beside me. Sometimes you give me such a scare it makes my heart tear. Into my eyes, you give me a deadly stare. In you I put no trust, this circumstance have me crushed. To sneak and get away I'll rush. When you near, I fear.

By: Brittani Darensbourg

Shy

In a moment, you caught my eye. I didn't have the words to express or find. You completely blew my mind. Romantic thoughts of us having dinner with sweet wine. Wishing and hoping one day I can make you all mine. Not being able to approach you is very pitiful but true. I'm into you, I am not gonna lie but I remain..... shy.

By: Brittani Darensbourg

I Wonder

Do you still care? Or was it all just a love affair? I always thought we were the perfect pair. Tell me, I brought you pleasure or pain? Or did our love go down the drain? Many mixed thoughts, feeling like I'm going insane. Are we meant to be? Or am I better off free? I wonder.....

By: Brittani Darensbourg

Envy

Hatred towards me because of the success I've achieved. Negative vibes I receive because of you lacking self-esteem and in yourself you don't believe. Jealousy that turns into rage, you and I will never be similar or on the same page. Your mind and heart will always be trapped and caged, until you change your wicked ways. Wishing evil on me cause of my good looks, on the edge I'm being pushed. You're not friendly, of me you envy.

By: Brittani Darensbourg

Disappointed

Many decisions I've made in my life wasn't always right. Not all days are sunny and bright. A lot of negative mixed thoughts keep me up at night. Trying to stay positive is hard to fight. Wishing I could start over and do it wise. Making better choices in the future will cause me to rise. By GOD, I need to be anointed then I wouldn't be….. disappointed.

By: Brittani Darensbourg

Prideful

*E*xcessive confidence presented with high quality evidence. Expect nothing less but the best. Insisting on looking down on others and the rest. Constantly putting yourself on a higher level, proof of evilness and serving the devil. Of your ways and thoughts be mindful, its bad to be prideful.

By: Brittani Darensbourg

Lust

A powerful desire, sets your physical being on fire. Deeply crave for needs you won't believe. An intense connection that fulfills short term dreams. An imitated love emotion that leads to destruction, that causes corruption. Knowing this dangerous feeling is a must, damaged souls caused by lust.

By: Brittani Darensbourg

Greed

Nothing is never enough. Continually want everything in a rush. Always have the best of things, Arrogance is what it brings. Constantly chasing for more, losing what's important is what you heading for. Feening for wants more than needs, full of greed.

By: Brittani Darensbourg

Crave

As for time, so much of it I try to save. A lot to each other, we gave. Now our fairytale love story is in the grave. I find myself sad many days, to stand alone, I am strong and brave. Moments I wish the feelings would go away and my emotions would behave. It's only fair to say, it's you that I still..... Crave.

By: Brittani Darensbourg

Wrath

Extreme anger inside my mind, putting my heart in a bind. Bitterness and strong resentment from the past, these emotions won't go away fast. Revenge is always my first thought, not the last. Won't ever get over it negativity still bound up a bit. Bad experiences took me down the wrong path. I'm full of wrath.

By: Brittani Darensbourg

Vengeance

*E*very time I think of you, I'm in complete anger. Having you present will be complete danger. No care in my heart for you like a complete stranger. This is the worst I've ever been betrayed and felt played. Somehow in some way your payback will be on the way. These thoughts and feelings doesn't feel rare. Picturing myself looking in your eyes with a dark stare. My prayers must be full of repentance, because my heart is full of..... vengeance.

By: Brittani Darensbourg

Part II

GOOD EMOTIONS

Peace

A beautiful sound of wind blowing the ocean waves. The sky so bright with perfect colored sun rays. Together we stand, holding hands. On this lovely land, knowing god is in our plan. To love you unconditionally, I can. Being beside you makes all my worries decrease. You bring me so much peace.....

By: Brittan Darensbourg

Admire

One hot summer day, there was a man that made me feel right in every way. Captivated and infatuated by his flaming biceps with skin that glows so right as the sun light. Eyes that are aquamarine green like the ocean waves, is it really him that my heart craves? A physical attraction fantasy making my emotions weak. My eyes won't let me just take a peak. Looking at you sets my soul on fire, everything I desire. Yes, you are the man that I admire.

By: Brittani Darensbourg

Happiness

$\mathcal{S}$teamy sensations of your gentle touch, being so close to you I enjoy so much. As I lay down staring in your eyes, I realize all the joy you bring me by surprise. Comfortable and safe knowing you're all mine. Intimacy that brings me to ecstasy. My heart has no heaviness, because of you..... You bring me so much happiness.

By: Brittani Darensbourg

Surprise

You always there for me no matter if its sunshine or storm. Your heart is a special charm. To you, I won't ever do no harm. In your presence I don't have to be warn. Being by your side makes my spirit rise. You are a blessing in disguise, taken by surprise.

By: Brittani Darensbourg

Inspiration

You're who I look up to on a daily basis. Won't ever try to compete or run races. Difficult battles endured forced you to live life in many phases. Through the trials and the pain, you never change. It's more than admiration, you're my..... inspiration.

By: Brittani Darensbourg
Dedicated to my mother, Jada

Grateful

*N*ever always had what I wanted. But I refuse to let my mind be haunted. Having a heart full of gratitude with a great attitude. Giving thanks every day I wake. Not a minute of life for granted I take. Moments when I rest, I look up to the sky knowing god is the reason I'm blessed. Very graceful but forever..... grateful.

By: Brittani Darensbourg

Sympathy

I know its been rough. Keeping a positive mindset is not enough, It's never easy taking a lost. Drowning in tears and sorrow will be a huge cost. The happy moments will never go down the drain, Knowing they won't be repeated is a huge amount of pain, Your feelings won't match my empathy, but you have my deepest sympathy.

By: Brittani Darensbourg

www.ingramcontent.com/pod-product-compliance
Lightning Source LLC
Chambersburg PA
CBHW040902110726
48005CB00001B/170